Jorge Lorenzo

Portrait of a Champion

Jorge Lorenzo

Portrait of a Champion

First published in May 2011

British Library Cataloguing in Publication Data

A catalogue record for this book is available from the British Library

ISBN 978 0 85733 095 6

Library of Congress Control No. 2011924023

Published by Haynes Publishing,
Sparkford, Yeovil, Somerset BA22 7JJ, UK

Tel: 01963 442030 Fax: 01963 440001
Int. tel: +44 1963 442030 Int. fax: +44 1963 440001
E-mail: sales@haynes.co.uk
Website: www.haynes.co.uk

Haynes North America Inc.
861 Lawrence Drive, Newbury Park,
California 91320, USA

Printed in the USA by Odcombe Press LP,
1299 Bridgestone Parkway, La Vergne, TN 37086

Photographs: Getty Images (Mirco Lazzari) except pages 7 to 15 (personal files) and page 155 (courtesy of newspaper ABC)

Design and layout: dtm+tagstudy (www.tagstudy.es)

Published in association with Scyla Editores, S. A., Spain

Prologue

By Jorge Lorenzo

Putting together a photo book charting every step of your career is not something you get to do every day. I am really excited that this book has been made available to racing fans and to the general public. When Haynes suggested the idea last year I didn't need to think about it twice. For me it is not a matter of financial gain but a nice keepsake for people who love motorcycle racing and have been following my career, no matter how long for – whether they started yesterday or back in 2002 when I made my debut in 125cc.

At the start of this year I called my mother to ask her a favour: "Mum, do you remember those photos you've got of me as a kid? If you've still got them tucked away somewhere please can you dig them out and send them to me?" My mum laughed but I could tell she was a little worried too. "Will you remember to give them back?" she asked. "Yes of course, don't worry!" I told her. "I wouldn't lose something like this."

So from then on we were able to start compiling this photographic autobiography, with a first chapter of pictures of when I was a baby, playing with my sister and my friends, riding trials and motocross, sliding around the car park at Aquacity and then competing in the Spanish and European Championships.

The rest have come from the library at Getty Images or from a professional file I keep on all the events I go to. It has been a long process, but an enjoyable one that has allowed me to relive some of the greatest moments of my 24-year-old life.

Matt Roberts has been working with me all winter, organising the photos we would need for the 240 pages that make up the book before going through them with myself and my team so that we could decide what we wanted to use. Matt came to Barcelona at the start of February and we sat down and went through every single page together. We like it and my personal hope is that you enjoy every single photo as much as the last.

I also hope there are more books to come in the future. This would mean that all the hard work we are doing is taking us in the right direction.

01

First
steps

These photos bring back a lot of great memories. I had a fun and busy childhood – whether I was at home riding trial and dirt bikes in Mallorca, on holiday in Galicia or starting out in the early days of my racing career in Barcelona. I remember all of these times with great fondness.

In search of a dream

From the age of three my goal was to become MotoGP World Champion. My father taught me everything I know, starting on the wastelands near my home in Palma de Mallorca and in the car park of a local waterpark, where I used to put on a show for the English and German tourists. I loved the limelight and I soon had to get used to it as my hobby quickly turned into a career.

▲ My first year in the Copa Aprilia in 1997. My dad had to get special permission for me to ride because I was only ten years old and the minimum age was 12. I think I qualified third and finished seventh in the wet in my first race at Cartagena.

▲ (Above) By 1999 I was the correct age and managed to win the Copa Aprilia – you can already recognise my riding style (number 48)!

▲ (Above right) We always had to pull the clutch in at the end of the race and save the engine so they could inspect it. (Below) On the podium with Angel Rodríguez and Joan Olivé at Jarama in 1998.

▶ My first win on the international stage in the European Championship, in Braga, Portugal 2001. That is Dovizioso in third place, the early days of a long-lasting rivalry!

◀ This is the second evolution of this haircut. The first one had stripes down the side and a big J shaved into the back! I loved it – especially seeing people's faces when I took my helmet off!

The sweet taste of success

My performances in the Copa Aprilia had caught the eye of Dani Amatriaín, an experienced former racer and manager of the Monlau Competición racing team. In 1997 we were short of cash but my father sent Dani a video of me riding at home in Mallorca and persuaded him to take a chance and sign me up. We moved to Barcelona and in 2000 I progressed to the Spanish Championship with his team – again with special permission from the authorities because I was too young.

◄ In my first season in the Spanish Championship I scored a best result of sixth and finished 18th in the championship, but in 2001 I managed two podium finishes and a pole position. On the right I am with Hector Faubel and Angel Rodríguez at Valencia, already sucking my famous Chupa Chups!

▼ It took me about a year to learn how to ride a Grand Prix bike. I was so small that I couldn't reach the gear-shifter properly and used to shift around 1,000rpm too early so as not to destabilise the bike. I was quick through the corners but lost a lot of time down the straights.

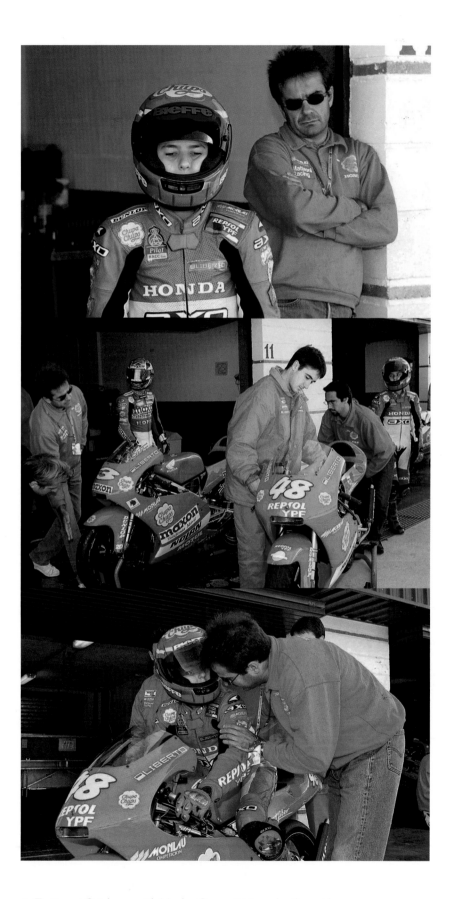

▲ Testing at Catalunya with Monlau Competición under the guidance of Dani Amatriaín. My team-mate was Toni Elías (middle picture) and I learned a lot about riding a 125 by following him in practice.

02

The world awaits

The 2002 season

My World Championship
career started on my 15th
birthday – the second day
of the Spanish Grand Prix at
Jerez. I was a very ambitious
kid who was desperate to get
out on track and race. I had
only won a couple of races in
the European Championship
but Dani had convinced Derbi
to give me a chance and I
was able to make my World
Championship debut at
the earliest opportunity,
although this time there was
no special dispensation for
my age! It was a tough year
because the bike wasn't very
competitive and I wasn't
really ready to fight with
such strong opposition.

Grand Prix of Catalonia

16 June
Circuit de Catalunya | Catalunya

▼ My first 'home' Grand Prix at Barcelona was a good weekend for me. I qualified on the second row for the first time and scored my first World Championship points in 14th place. Here I am leading Mattia Angeloni (84) and Stefano Perugini (7), who passed me for 13th with four laps to go.

Grand Prix of Italy

2 June
Mugello | Italy

▲ The track looks huge compared to the little 125 and that's how it felt too! In fact, everything felt bigger!

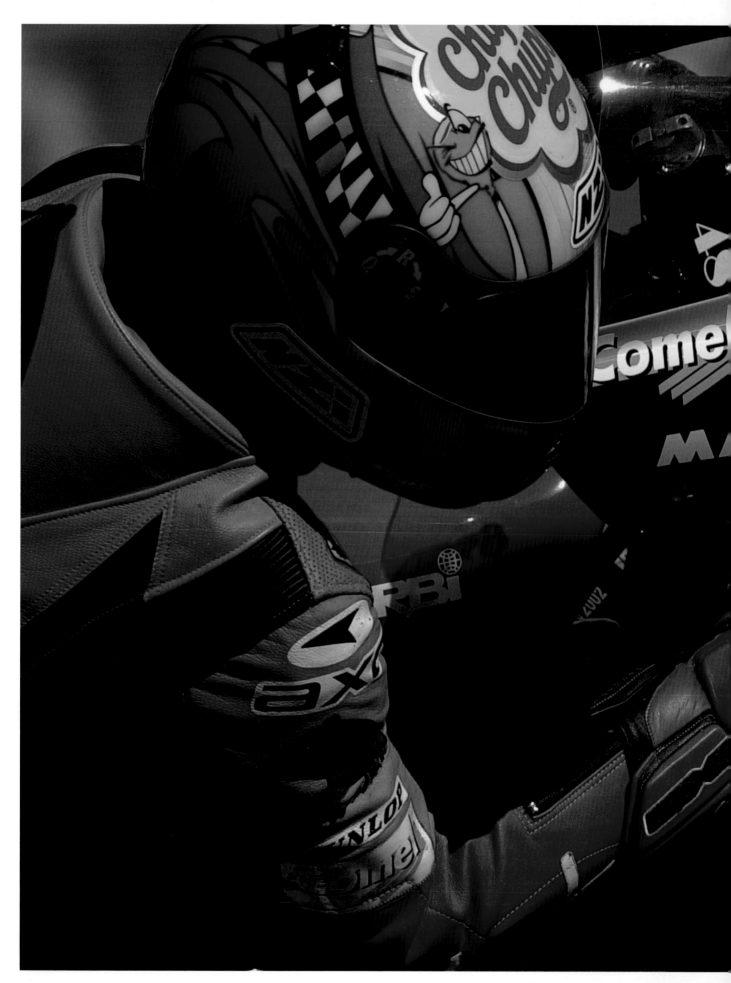

"2002 was a tough year because the bike wasn't very competitive and I wasn't really ready to fight with such strong opposition."

Grand Prix of Germany

**21 July
Sachsenring | Germany**

▼ As you can see I had a few problems in the next race at Sachsenring – I qualified 17th but only finished 19th. It is a difficult circuit to learn and I still haven't got the hang of it. It is the only circuit on the current calendar, apart from Aragon, where I have never won.

Grand Prix of Great Britain

**14 July
Donington Park | Great Britain**

▲ Donington Park was a much harder race than Barcelona but a better result. I went from 21st on the grid to finish 13th and was starting to close the gap to the group at the front.

Grand Prix of Czech Republic

25 August
Automotodrom Brno | Czech Republic

▲ Reacquainting myself with an old rival: Dovi and I battle for
20th place at Brno. I beat him by less than two tenths of
a second but it wasn't a result I was happy with.

Grand Prix of Portugal

8 September
Estoril | Portugal

◀ Red and green: the colours of Portugal and the colours of my bike! Little did I know that in the future it would become a talismanic country for me.

▼ This picture must have been taken during practice because the race took place in torrentially wet conditions. I qualified 25th and crashed out on the seventh lap, but, to be fair, only 14 riders finished.

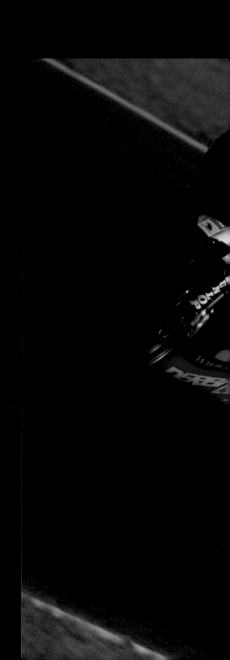

and Prix of Valencia
3 November
Cheste | Valencia

Marco Simoncelli crashing out of the fight with me and Nobby Ueda in turn one. He was a combative rider even then and we would have a few more encounters at Valencia in the years ahead. Ueda also crashed but I finished way back in a disappointing 22nd.

The 2003 Season

The 2003 season started off in much the same way as 2002 ended. I had the same problems with the set-up of the Derbi but I couldn't express myself to the mechanics – I just got frustrated. Sometimes I was fast but I didn't understand why, the same when I was slow. The big turning point was Juanito Llansa joining as my mechanic – he eventually made me realise it was me that needed to change, not the bike.

Grand Prix of South Africa

 27 April
Phakisa Freeway | South Africa

▲ The start of a new season in South Africa. Leading future 125cc World Champions Mike di Meglio (63) and Álvaro Bautista (19), but outside the top 20. I guess we all had a lot to learn. You can see the frustration on my face after the race.

◀ Another early encounter with Simoncelli. He beat me in this race, finishing 20th. I was 24th. To be honest, I never thought we would end up racing each other in MotoGP but it has happened in a relatively short space of time. Sometimes it doesn't seem like it, but riders develop very quickly.

Grand Prix of Italy

8 June
Mugello | Italy

▼ Mugello is always a tough race for a 125cc rider near the back because there are so many wildcards looking to make a name for themselves. Here I am fighting with Simone Corsi (24) and Thomas Lüthi (12) for a points-scoring finish.

▶ I eventually crashed out of this race with just a couple of laps to go when I was in 14th place. I was furious! I didn't know it then but Mugello would later become an extremely important circuit in my life.

Grand Prix of Great Britain

13 July
Donington Park | Great Britain

▲ After Mugello we went to Catalunya and scored a fantastic sixth place, but then I crashed out again in the next two races at Assen and Donington Park. This shot was actually taken during a promo session for Derbi.

Grand Prix of Portugal

7 September
Estoril | Portugal

I qualified third after following Dani Pedrosa for a lap, securing my first front-row start. A couple of weeks earlier I raced in the CEV at Jarama and I won, which gave me a lot of self-confidence and motivation, and then we had a test at Almería, where I had a big head-to-head with Juanito. From that point on things suddenly began to look brighter. I spent the whole of this race running with the front group but then they dropped me and I finished up fighting with Gabor Talmacsi (79). It was a hugely important race for me because I only finished eight seconds behind the winner and I realised I could compete with these guys. At the front you can see Stefano Perugini (7), Steve Jenkner (17) and Alex de Angelis (15), who were combative riders – I had to quickly learn to fight them back.

Grand Prix of Brazil

 20 September
Nelson Piquet | Riol

▼ Shortly after Estoril we went to Rio and even though I hadn't finished on a Grand Prix podium I managed to take my first win! It was an incredible race but I was so confident. In fact, this was where I executed the 'X-Fuera' move for the first time – around the outside of Casey Stoner and Dani Pedrosa for the lead! This is still the most amazing feeling I have had in my career – I'll never forget it. At just 16 years and 139 days I became the second youngest Grand Prix winner of all time, behind Marco Melandri.

Grand Prix of Japan

5 October
Motegi | Pacific

◀ Unfortunately my first win didn't stop me from crashing a lot. This was in the race at Motegi. I had fought back from 12th on the first lap to second place with five laps to go, setting what would prove to be the fastest lap of the race – the first of my career – on the way through. I was only a second behind Dovizioso at the front and I could sense my second win!

▼ Coming into the chicane at the end of the lap I ran far too tight through the corner. The 'steps' on the rumble strip get higher the closer to the inside of the corner you are and I was at their highest point. The wheel got damaged and the front immediately folded, causing me to crash.

Grand Prix of Malaysia

12 October
Sepang Circuit | Malaysia

▲ Fighting with Mika Kallio (36) and Casey Stoner (27) for second place at Sepang – Dani Pedrosa had escaped at the front. Casey crashed or retired quite early and I held off Mika for most of the race, but he beat me on the last lap. Anyway, this was my second podium of the season and also my first pole position.

"During 2003 I finally realised it was me that needed to change, not the bike."

▼ The season got off to a bad start. I qualified 13th but lost positions
in the race and crossed the line in 16th, missing out on the points.

The 2004 season

The 2004 season started out the same way as 2002 and 2003: badly! I didn't score a point for the first two races but in the third I finished on the podium. Over the course of the season we became much more consistent – I went on to score seven podiums in total, with three wins, and finished fourteenth in the championship. I had spent two seasons adapting to the Derbi and now I knew exactly how to ride it: by carrying lots of speed into and through the corners and getting on the gas as soon as possible. Some top quality riders had tried and failed, including a World Champion, but now we could play fully to its strengths.

Grand Prix of Spain

 2 May
Jerez | Spain

▲ My home Grand Prix at Jerez was another one to forget. I qualified 14th but then lost ten places at the start and crashed out after three laps trying to recover.

Grand Prix of France

 16 May
Le Mans | France

▼ Before this race Juanito told me a stupid story about a guy who made his lazy camel run by smashing a pair of stones around its balls! If the camel didn't run he showed it the stones! At Le Mans Juanito took two stones out of the gravel and showed them to me. It worked!

Grand Prix of Italy
6 June
Mugello | Italy

▼ I was keen to follow up my podium in France with another finish. I qualified eighth at Mugello and crossed the line in tenth – it wasn't a brilliant result but I was starting to realise that sometimes it is better to stay on the bike, take the points and move on to the next race.

Dutch TT
26 June
Assen | Netherlands

▶ Along with Rio 2003 this is probably one of the best and most famous races of my career. I led virtually the whole race but made a mistake on the last lap and was passed by three or four riders. Within a couple of corners I was back up to second and then with two corners to go I passed Locatelli for the win. Those last-lap battles in 125cc were like a heart attack! Interestingly four of the five riders in the lead group that day are now in MotoGP: Dovizioso, Stoner, Barberá and myself.

Grand Prix of Brazil

 4 July
Nelson Piquet | Rio

◀ Riding my bike through the paddock in Brazil. I was happy and confident at this point because I had won here the previous year but in the race I tried to repeat my 'X-Fuera' move in the same corner on Stoner and crashed! I wrecked my fingers and still have the scars to show for it.

▼ I was so disappointed because I had qualified third fastest and I really wanted to repeat my debut success. It was a track I loved and to end up in hospital was the worst way to sign off from it, because since 2004 we have never been back to Brazil. I would love to ride there again in MotoGP.

Grand Prix of Germany

18 July
Sachsenring | Germany

▲ This was the next race after Brazil and my fingers were still a mess. They were covered in bandages and I had to have specially made large gloves to fit over them. I had a good race considering how much discomfort I was in, finishing sixth and just over a second off the race winner.

Grand Prix of Great Britain

🇬🇧 **25 July**
Donington Park | Great Britain

▲ Another podium at Donington with two familiar faces! Dovizioso was in a different league that day and he won the race easily from Bautista. I made a bad start and was down in seventh on the first lap, but I fought through and won a late battle with Mika Kallio for third.

Grand Prix of Czech Republic

22 August
Automotodrom Brno | Czech Republic

▼ Victory at Max Biaggi's talismanic circuit! A quick story about Max: he was my hero and as a surprise on my 15th birthday at Jerez I was taken to his motorhome to meet him. It was a very special moment for me and we spoke for ten minutes. I can't quite remember what he said about Valentino though...

Grand Prix of Portugal

5 September
Estoril | Portugal

◄ Third place by less than a tenth of a second ahead of Pablo Nieto at Estoril. I had put my early problems at the Portuguese circuit behind me but it still wasn't one of my favourites. This was the first time in my career I scored three podiums in a row.

Grand Prix of Japan

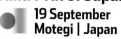

**19 September
Motegi | Japan**

◀ This was a disastrous weekend for us, in practice and in the race, which I remember was stopped because of a spectacular crash on the front straight. Here I am behind Kallio (36) before he crashed. I went on to finish seventh.

Grand Prix of Qatar

2 October
Losail Circuit | Qatar

▲ My third win of the 2004 season. Not only did this race make history as the first ever motorcycle Grand Prix in Qatar, but it was also the closest-ever finish.

◄ Andrea Dovizioso and I took the chequered flag at the same time and I became the first rider ever to win by 0.000 seconds! It was a photo finish decided by Race Direction and when I crossed the line I had no idea who had won.

Grand Prix of Malaysia
10 October
Sepang Circuit | Malaysia

▲ This is where my chances of finishing runner-up in the championship virtually disappeared. The engine broke halfway through the race and I went absolutely ballistic in the garage. I threw my helmet, pushed all the panels over... wrecked the place basically! I was way out of line.

▶ It is funny thinking back to that day in Malaysia. I couldn't have imagined then that only six years later I would be back there celebrating the MotoGP World Championship title. It seems crazy thinking about it now!

Grand Prix of Australia
17 October
Phillip Island | Australia

▲ Phillip Island was always a great circuit for a 125cc machine. I remember the race was a three-way battle with Dovizioso and Stoner. On the penultimate lap I let them pass me for the lead, planning an attack out of the final corner. I got myself into second place on the last lap behind Dovi but Stoner made a move on me and wrecked my plan! I took second in a photo finish with Casey.

Grand Prix of Valencia

31 October
Circuito Ricardo Tormo | Valencia

▼ I still had a chance of finishing runner-up in the championship in the final race at Valencia but only if I won. I told my dad before the race that I was either going to win or crash ... unfortunately it was the latter. Below you can see me fighting for second place with Bautista (19), Gino Borsoi (23) and Pablo Nieto. I would leave 125cc with a record of four wins, three poles, three fastest laps and nine podiums from 46 races across three seasons.

The 2005 Season

The end of 2004 and the start of 2005 was a very busy time. I had various offers: to stay in 125 but with Aprilia, to go to 250 with Dani Amatriaín's team, Honda and Fortuna

MotoGP with Tech3 Yamaha. I was still only 17 so I was nowhere near ready to ride a 990cc MotoGP bike and I didn't want to waste another year in 125 – so it was an easy choice.

▲ I made a decent start to th
at Jerez, taking sixth place
pressure was already mour
the Spanish press and fans
were keen to build up my ri

I was still only 17 so I was nowhere near ready to ride a 990cc MotoGP bike and I didn't want to waste another year in 25 – so it was an easy choice."

Grand Prix of Portugal

 17 April
Estoril | Portugal

▲ Amazingly, when I see this picture I think about my first girlfriend, Eva. We had been chatting over the internet for two years but it was after this race when she sent me a text message for the first time and I knew she was interested in me! I finished tenth but I didn't care!

Grand Prix of France

15 May
Le Mans | France

▲ You can't take this line any more!
The exit from the final turn at Le Mans
used to have this rumbled tarmac on
the outside but now they have changed
it to artificial grass, which is not quite
as grippy.

▶ This was a decent weekend for me. I
qualified on the front row and stayed
with the lead group for the first half
before dropping back and finishing fifth.
It was a bit like the 125 race at Estoril in
2003: I was starting to show signs of
my speed in the category.

Grand Prix of Italy

5 June
Mugello | Italy

▲ Just like going from Estoril to Rio in 2003, I went into the next race after Le Mans and scored my first podium. I finished second to Dani Pedrosa at Mugello following an exciting battle on the last lap with de Angelis, passing him with just a couple of corners left in front of his home crowd.

"Montmeló was
a disaster for me.
I was fastest in

Dutch TT

25 June
Assen | Netherlands

▲ A week and a half after an operation to fix my collarbone I came back at Assen and set pole position. On the track, at least, it was light at the end of the tunnel of one of the toughest periods of my professional life so far.

▶ The race was really physical because I was at the front throughout, chased by Pedrosa and Sebastian Porto (19). After all my hard work they both passed me and pulled out half a second on the last lap. At the time I felt cheated but really I had been naïve.

The 2006 Season

At the end of 2005 we accepted a big-money offer to switch to Aprilia. We knew that the bike, with its corner speed, would be more suited to my style than the Honda. I'd spent the whole 2005 season struggling to tuck in behind the fairing but now I had room to spare. Unfortunately I got carried away and I was knocked unconscious and broke my collarbone again in a heavy crash on the second day of testing at Valencia. We had new mechanics but it was essentially the same team, with Héctor Barberá (80) again as my team-mate.

26 March
Jerez | Spain

◄ The first day I rode the bike after my collarbone operation I was already faster than on the Honda and I had no trouble winning the first race at Jerez. It was my first win at 'The Cathedral' of Spanish racing in any class.

Grand Prix of Qatar
8 April
Losail Circuit | Qatar

▼ We won the second race at Qatar and in the press they were saying it was all because of my psychologist Joaquín Dosail, who we had worked with since 2005. I felt he was taking too much credit so we split with him after this race.

Grand Prix of Italy
4 June
Mugello | Italy

▲ After parting from Dosail I had a disastrous few weeks, crashing in Turkey, finishing fourth in China, crashing again at Le Mans and, worse than all of this, falling out with my father and breaking up with my girlfriend. At Mugello I met Alex Debón, who raced as my team-mate as a wildcard, and he did an incredible job to help me win the race and turn my season around. These photos remind me of so many emotions because a race lasts just 45 minutes but each day was 24 hours long.

Grand Prix of Catalunya

▼ The majority of things happening in my life at the time were negative but on the track at least everything was positive. The sweetest thing I could taste was that Chupa Chups on the podium and after Mugello I took a second place in Barcelona after a great fightback.

Grand Prix of Great Britain

2 July
Donington Park | Great Britain

▼ We were going from strength to strength and after Barcelona I scored back-to-back wins at Assen and Donington Park – both of them from pole position. My confidence and concentration were back, having been so badly shattered since the crash in Istanbul.

Grand Prix of Czech Republic

 20 August
Automotodrom Brno | Czech Republic

▲ Brno was my sixth win of the season and my sixth consecutive podium. I now
led the championship by seven points from Dovizioso having trailed by 29 after
Le Mans just six races previously.

Grand Prix of Malaysia

10 September
Sepang Circuit | Malaysia

▼ Our winning run continued at Sepang. You can see that my reaction looks aggressive and over-confident, but really I was still a very shy young man. It was like a mask – a false image I was trying to give people – of strength and ambition. Some people didn't understand and saw it in a negative light.

Grand Prix of Australia

 **17 September**
Phillip Island | Australia

▲ The top one is a funny photo – it looks like I'm being held aloft by the
Australian fans! In the race I fought with Dovizioso (34) in the early laps
but something happened to him at the end and he dropped back, giving
us a good points advantage. In the end I won the race by just 0.009
seconds from de Angelis.

Grand Prix of Japan

24 September
Motegi | Japan

▼ Going into the final three races of the season I had a 24-point advantage over Dovi so I knew that if I could keep him behind me in each race I would win the title. I managed that at Motegi, the home of Honda, finishing third with him in fourth after a tough but important race.

Grand Prix of Portugal

15 October
Estoril | Portugal

◀ Estoril was my first mathematical chance to wrap up the title and I remember a lot of Spanish journalists made the trip over the border. All I had to do was beat Dovi but I was slow all weekend. I was feeling the pressure, I crashed a couple of times and the race was in the damp ... it was butt-clenching!

Grand Prix of Valencia

29 October
Comunitat Valenciana | Valencia

▲ I finished fifth in Portugal but Dovi won so it went to the last round at Valencia. I was nervous because I now needed to finish in the top four to make sure of the title. After everything we had been through I couldn't bear the thought of losing it all in the last race, but after a tense start Debón helped me again and I was able to win my first title.

"After everything we had been through I couldn't bear the thought of losing it all in the last race."

The 2007 Season

In 2007 I was much more consistent. I won one more race than in 2006 (nine compared to eight) but also I only failed to finish one race, which was an important step because Andrea Dovizioso was a strong rival once again, ready to pounce on any mistakes. Overall I crashed less and began to enjoy myself a lot more, coming up with some entertaining celebrations too...

Grand Prix of Qatar

 **10 March**
Losail Circuit | Qatar

◀ I remember turning up in Qatar for the final test, a week before the start of the season, and I was totally overweight! I had been enjoying myself too much at various galas and presentations over the winter and eating badly. I weighed 64kg, compared to my 'fighting weight' of 59 or 60kg, and had chubby cheeks. I ended the test two seconds off the pace set by Bautista, who was a rookie. We turned the bike upside-down but nothing worked. After that I stayed in Qatar and spent three or four hours in the gym every day, training hard and hardly eating. I lost four kilos in a week and I was hungry – for food and for success! I took two seconds off my lap times and won the race.

Grand Prix of Spain

 25 March
Jerez | Spain

▼ We took my new body and new confidence back to Spain for round two at Jerez, where I set pole position (below) and won the race (above) by just 0.2 seconds from my compatriot and old rival Bautista.

Grand Prix of China

6 May
Shanghai Circuit | China

▲ Lorenzo's Land! This was actually the second time I did this celebration – the first was in the previous race at Jerez. I had been trying to think of something original for a while and then one day in the gym Marcos said to me "What kind of a conqueror doesn't have a flag?" The logo was easy, my 'X-Fuera' symbol, and the words 'Lorenzo's Land' in English so they could be understood around the world.

Grand Prix of France

20 May
Le Mans | France

▼ Being followed by my old team-mate Héctor Barberá in practice ... again! This used to really wind me up and he knew it, which made him do it more. We fell out over it in 2005 and didn't speak for over a year! We were young and competitive but I don't think he's a bad person and as a rider he's got real talent.

"I lost four kilos in a week and I was hungry – for food and for success!"

Grand Prix of Italy

3 June
Mugello | Italy

▲ I love pulling wheelies – it was something my father insisted I practise from a young age. He said it was important, to put on a show for the tourists who used to watch me at Aquacity but also because it gives you a lot of control over the bike. I remember I had a little pushbike and my father told me if I could do a wheelie and pedal 20 times with the front wheel in the air he would buy me one of these little caps with a fan on the front! I loved those caps so I practised and practised through the whole summer until finally I did it. This picture must have been taken during practice because the race was a disaster – I got knocked off by Bautista.

Grand Prix of Catalunya
10 June
Circuit de Catalunya | Catalunya

▶ By the middle of 2007 I was starting to get more and more inventive with my celebrations. This one after my victory at Montmeló was a tribute to my favourite rock band: the Red Hot Chilli Peppers.

Grand Prix of Great Britain
24 June
Donington Park | Great Britain

▼ I remember this race with special fondness because I always used to have problems in the wet, but I rode well in this one until I crashed. I had done some dirt-track training with Kenny Roberts at his ranch pre-season and it really helped my wet-weather riding. Unfortunately on this occasion Dovi won and pulled a lot of points back.

Dutch TT

30 June
Assen | Netherlands

▲ I bounced back at Assen with a win from pole position, just as I had done the year before. Unfortunately neither of these performances makes up for my disappointment from 2005, which is the overriding memory of my 250cc career at the Dutch TT.

▶ Assen is still one of my favourite circuits in the world so I enjoyed planting the Lorenzo's Land flag there. Most importantly, this win gave me a 23-point lead over Dovizioso in the championship, recovering a lot of the points we had lost at Donington.

Grand Prix of Germany

 15 July
Sachsenring | Germany

▲ I was still struggling to get to grips with Sachsenring and could only manage fourth in this race, although I was only half a second behind the winner (Hiroshi Aoyama) and crucially Dovi was behind me in fifth.

Grand Prix of USA

 22 July
Mazda Raceway | United States

◀ There was no 250cc race at Laguna Seca but I went with a double mission. The first was very public: to commentate on the race for Spanish television. The second was very secret: to sign a contract with Yamaha to ride in MotoGP in 2008.

Grand Prix of San Marino

2 September
Misano | San Marino

▲ As part of my mental preparation in 2007 I was watching a lot of inspirational films, like 'Gladiator' and '300' – films about honour, respect and courage, which are values I share. Also an Italian television commentator had started calling me 'The Spaniard', after the character played by Russell Crowe. So for Mugello we thought it would be

Grand Prix of Portugal
 16 September
Estoril | Portugal

▼ Another third place at Estoril, a circuit I still didn't like and would now never win at in the smaller classes – although I was happy with this result. Remarkably, just seven months later I would be back there in very different circumstances and with a very different opinion of the track.

Grand Prix of Japan

23 September
Motegi | Japan

▲ Another tough race in mixed conditions. Again, don't be fooled by the wheelie. I had a terrible race and could only manage 11th place, with Dovizioso coming second. Once again I found myself in the position of having dominated the season but with the possibility of losing out on the title because of a couple of bad results. It was a frustrating weekend.

Grand Prix of Malaysia

21 October
Sepang Circuit | Malaysia

▶ Thankfully we recovered with a win in
Australia and third place in Malaysia,
and those results sealed the title for me.
Having started the season training like
Rocky Balboa and trying to recover the
eye of the tiger, there was only one way
to celebrate!

"Once again I found myself in the position of having dominated the season but with the possibility of losing out on the title because of a couple of bad results."

03

The move to MotoGP

egotiations with Yamaha ad been on-going since 2006, hen we made a pre-contract greement, but we finally ut pen to paper during the IotoGP round at Laguna Seca he following July. We had two ecret test sessions that August, t Almería and Brno, and I dapted quickly. After six years Grand Prix and with two 250cc titles, I felt it was the right time to move up and I couldn't have been doing it in a better team, alongside Valentino Rossi. Marcos told me "Valentino had better not retire yet because to be a true champion you have to beat him!" I was happy with what I had achieved so far but this is where my story really starts.

Grand Prix of Qatar

9 March
Losail Circuit | Qatar

It was incredible to set pole position for my first race in the premier class. Two months previously I had been two seconds off the pace in the test at Sepang and this was unthinkable. I was in a really positive frame of mind and had just been envisaging this result. I went on to finish second behind Stoner – an amazing start to my rookie season.

Grand Prix of Spain

30 March
Jerez | Spain

▶ Three weeks later at Jerez I set pole again – the first rookie ever to do so in the first two races – and finished third. I couldn't really understand why I was going so well. I didn't know if it was simply because we had a good package or because the other riders were still sleeping – or if the level just wasn't as high as I'd expected!

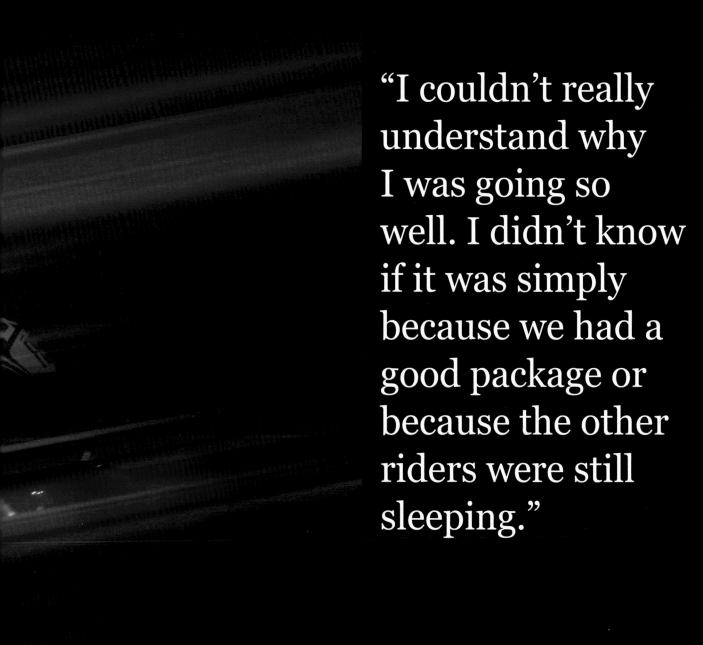

"I couldn't really understand why I was going so well. I didn't know if it was simply because we had a good package or because the other riders were still sleeping."

Grand Prix of Portugal
13 April
Estoril | Portugal

▼ After Jerez we had a test that gave me a lot of confidence to take to Estoril. I set pole position and everything came together in the race – I couldn't believe how easily I was able to pass Pedrosa and Rossi and take the win. After three races I had three poles, three podiums, my first win and the MotoGP World Championship lead.

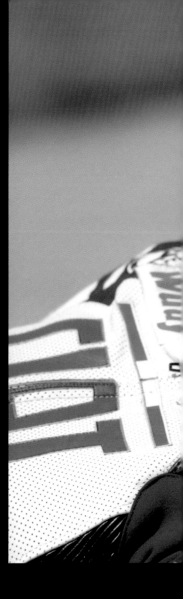

Grand Prix of China

4 May
Shanghai Circuit | China

▲ I was flying high – literally so in China! I was pushing too hard in first free practice and I had a huge crash – it was like in a computer game. I was in the air for more than a second and a half so I had time to think, 'Madre mía! This is going to hurt!' When I hit the tarmac I saw stars and started to feel a terrible pain in my ankles. I grabbed hold of them and started screaming, hoping it was just a dream.

Grand Prix of France
**18 May
Le Mans | France**

▲ I had fractures and ligament damage in both ankles but I went to France and rode. I crashed twice in practice and had a big moment when I went straight across the gravel at high speed in turn one. The crazy thing was that I had no fear of the bike at this point, I just thought the crashes had been bad luck. So despite the injuries I wasn't scared and even though it started to rain in the middle of the race I kept up my pace, passed Pedrosa and Colin Edwards, and finished second.

Grand Prix of Catalunya
8 June
Circuit de Catalunya | Catalunya

▼ Unfortunately fearlessness in MotoGP is not always a good thing. You can't keep crashing and get away with it. In practice at Montmeló I had the worst of my career, knocking myself unconscious and missing the race. An injury to your bones is one thing but when you damage your head and you can't remember anything for two or three days that is entirely different. Whenever I had crashed previously I had never thought how dangerous this sport could be but now I knew. Luckily, after three days I was okay again.

Grand Prix of Great Britain

22 June
Donington Park | Great Britain

▼ This is where the fear took hold. There were two weeks between Montmeló and Donington – too much time to think, for things to go round in your head, to think things you shouldn't. I started to believe that the crashes were my fault and when I eventually did get back out on track I decided to go more slowly, more carefully, but then I struggled to get back on the pace. At Donington I qualified down in 17th, although I came through to take sixth place.

Grand Prix of Germany

16 June
Sachsenring | Germany

▲ I finished sixth again at Assen and by Sachsenring I had started to recover my confidence. Slowly I was overcoming my fear of the bike, although I maintained my respect for it. I crashed out of the race but that was because of the rain. I would manage more poles and podiums before the end of the season but I would never recover the confidence I had in those first few races.

Grand Prix of United States
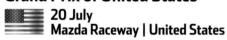 **20 July**
Mazda Raceway | United States

▲ I crashed out again at Laguna Seca, which was my lowest point of the season, but it was my mistake and I knew how it happened – not like at Le Mans or Montmeló. I thought I'd broken my leg but luckily it was not as serious as it looked. The worst thing was I missed my holidays! I spent a month in a cast and couldn't even take a bath. But this photo must have been taken in practice – things weren't so bad that I was lapping behind Anthony West (13) on the Kawasaki! Only joking Anthony!

Grand Prix of
Czech Republic

 **17 August
Automotodrom Brno
Czech Republic**

▶ When we came back from the
summer break my attitude had
changed. I was more positive and
I realised that I had to be more
relaxed, take it easier. I began to see
that if I did things more gradually I
was less likely to put myself at risk

Grand Prix of San Marino

31 August
Misano | San Marino

▲ We were having some problems with Michelin tyres but at Misano they worked well. I felt strong and I scored my first podium in six races, ending my longest dry spell since my first 125cc win in Rio.

◄ My schedule at a GP is really tight and I hardly get a moment to myself. However, I always make sure I have time to watch each practice session on DVD. I learn a lot from watching myself and the other riders.

Grand Prix of Indianapolis
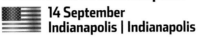
14 September
Indianapolis | Indianapolis

▼ It was fantastic to race for the first time at such a circuit as legendary as Indianapolis, although the race itself was extremely tough because of the tornado. I managed to score my first ever podium in the wet with third place although I could have finished second; they stopped the race just when I was closing on Nicky Hayden. It was a great experience and as always I enjoyed the support of the American fans.

Grand Prix of Japan

28 September
Motegi | Japan

▼ Until 2008 I didn't like Motegi but pole position there helped me recover my confidence. I felt it was all coming back to me and that I was riding really well again. Unfortunately in the race the tyres never gave me the opportunity to finish off the job but fourth place helped wrap up the constructors' title for Yamaha in front of their home fans.

Grand Prix of Australia

5 October
Phillip Island | Australia

▲ Riding a MotoGP bike for the first time at Phillip
Island was an incredible experience. I gradually and
carefully built up my speed over the weekend and
qualified second, but I could only manage fourth
in the race.

The 2009 Season

The big change for 2009, on the track at least, was the switch from Michelin tyres to Bridgestone. We had been handicapped throughout the 2008 season on the brakes and at some circuits we just weren't competitive,

so now it felt like we were on a level playing field. A lot had changed for me off the track too. I split with my manager Dani Amatriaín, with Marcos taking his place, and so dropped Dani's old number 48 in favour of the 99.

It was a fresh start and I was keen not to make the same mistakes as I had in the past. Pre-season testing was difficult, especially at first, as we got used to the new tyres, but I was confident we would quickly get up to speed.

Grand Prix of Qatar

 13 April
Losail Circuit | Qatar

◀ I still wasn't used to the Bridgestones in Qatar. Even though I knew what the secret was I still hadn't adapted my riding style 100 per cent and mentally I was uncertain. I didn't have the same conviction that I'd started the previous season with, and I made a lot of mistakes that night – it wasn't a great race for me and I finished third.

Grand Prix of Japan

 26 September
Motegi | Japan

▲ Motegi was better! It was a strange weekend because of the mixed weather and we took a couple of gambles with the tyres that paid off in the race, allowing me to take the win. The biggest factor though was my mental strength. I had been going to relaxation classes and they helped me stay focused despite the difficult conditions.

Grand Prix of Spain

▼ I was feeling confident after the win
in Japan but arrived at Jerez talking
too much. I was saying things about
Valentino in the press and even though
I was quick in practice, qualifying on
pole, I didn't back it up in the race,
eventually crashing when pushing
too hard to catch Stoner for a podium.
That was a big lesson.

Grand Prix of Catalunya

14 June
Circuit de Catalunya | Catalunya

▼ All my team behind me at Montmeló. Ironically it was my team-mate (not pictured!) who I should have been looking out for over my other shoulder in the final corner of the race! Not closing the door on Valentino in what has become one of the most famous moments in MotoGP history will always be one of the biggest regrets of my career.

Dutch TT

 27 June
Assen | Netherlands

◄ These photos surprised me when I first saw
them because I initially thought the top one was
of Pedrosa! I guess we are more similar than I
thought. To be honest I was starting to show my
more serious side by this point, concentrating
on being consistent and not making the same
mistakes as in 2008. At Assen I scored my
fourth podium in a row.

Grand Prix of Germany
19 July
Sachsenring | Germany

This was my best ever race at Sachsenring, finishing second to Valentino after another good battle with him – although ultimately it was another one that I wasn't able to win. Even though I was consistently on the podium, at this stage he was winning more races and edging clear in the championship.

Grand Prix of Czech Republic
16 August
Automotodrom Brno | Czech Republic

▼ The pressure was building and at Brno I cracked again. I had been the fastest in practice but lost ground early in the race and when I caught Valentino I tried to escape immediately, instead of waiting for the right moment. In one corner I braked 20 metres later and much harder than normal, and crashed. I don't regret it, though, because at the time I had to take a gamble on my title chances and that was the day to do it.

Grand Prix of Indianapolis

30 August
Indianapolis | Indianapolis

▲ I wasn't the only one cracking under pressure. The pendulum was swinging wildly and from being relatively close to the championship lead at Sachsenring, just 14 points behind, suddenly within two races the gap was 50. But at Indianapolis a crash for Valentino brought it back down to 25 and I had an outside chance again. Check out the Captain America helmet – one of my favourites!

Grand Prix of San Marino

 6 September
Misano | San Marino

▲ At Misano the pendulum swung back in favour of Rossi – he showed his best side that weekend at his home race. Not only did he win but he wore the 'Donkey' helmet and wore the ears onto the podium in reference to his mistake at Indy. It is one of the funniest celebrations I have seen him do and I laughed when I saw it. He is an expert at turning situations around in his favour – another thing I had to learn from him.

Grand Prix of Portugal

▼ The spaceman has landed: victory at Estoril for the second consecutive season. I love this picture because I almost look like a real astronaut, hanging on to the side of a rocket! All the fun livery aside, it was a really important win because Valentino finished fourth so it brought me back to within 28 points with three races left: an outside chance but still a chance.

Grand Prix of Australia

18 October
Phillip Island | Australia

◀ I remember I was ill in the week leading up to Phillip Island and I had a bad weekend. When we lined up on the grid I was weak and not properly focused. I was on the second row and tried too hard to take advantage of Nicky Hayden's slipstream. I got too close and ran us both off the track. My title hopes were almost over.

Grand Prix of Malaysia
25 October
Sepang Circuit | Malaysia

▲ Sepang was a disaster. Basically we had a problem starting my bike and we missed pit-lane closing, meaning we had to start from the back of the grid, which I think is a silly rule. I got a fantastic start, passed a couple of riders, then got lucky as a couple of others got tangled up with each other. I quickly caught Valentino and when he saw me I'm sure he said to himself that 'if Lorenzo can do it so I can I'. He latched onto my rear wheel and 'copied' my lines, building up his own rhythm to the point that he was able to pass me. I simply didn't have the pace to go with him this time and he was able to take a podium and the title.

Grand Prix of Qatar

11 April
Losail Circuit | Qatar

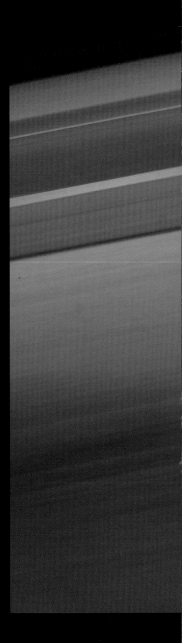

▶ Considering the shape we were in I was delighted to finish second in Qatar. I really felt the hours of gym work I'd missed out on pre-season and also the lack of laps on my M1. Everything was a struggle and I got tired quickly, which meant we couldn't get our set-up just right in practice. Still, everything came together on the night and we managed an almost perfect start to the season with second place.

Grand Prix of Valencia

8 November
Comunitat Valenciana | Valencia

▲ I was disappointed not to take the title fight to the final round, of course, but this had never been my objective for 2009. All I wanted was to improve on 2008 and I managed it: mission accomplished. Stoner's crash on the warm-up lap at Valencia guaranteed me the runner-up spot in the championship and I finished the season with another podium. Obviously if I were to improve on my championship position again in 2010 there was only one way to go...

The 2010 season

An injury during pre-season almost ruined my 2010 campaign before it started. In February I crashed riding motocross with Carlos Checa and some other friends at Montmeló and broke my hand. I felt the weight of the world on my shoulders. The fracture was really close to the scaphoid, which is a rider's worst nightmare. If you break that it is almost impossible to fix it and it has put a lot of riders into retirement, so I was very worried. I had an operation and we missed the second test at Sepang, and even though I made it for the final session in Qatar two weeks before the race I was in a lot of pain and needed constant physiotherapy. It was anything but a perfect start to the new season ahead.

Grand Prix of Spain

2 May
Jerez | Spain

▼ When we got to Jerez I was back to almost 100 per cent fitness. The weekend went well and even though I made a bad start I remained patient, waited for the bike to come to me – the opposite to 12 months previously! As my pace gathered Rossi and Pedrosa were slowing down. That gave me confidence and I knew I had to try. Dani rode really well but I was able to get past him at the end and win. It is one of my best ever races and one of my sweetest victories. Before the race I told the press there were two dreams that I wanted to turn into reality: to win at Jerez and to become MotoGP World Champion. The first one had now come true but the second would be more difficult.

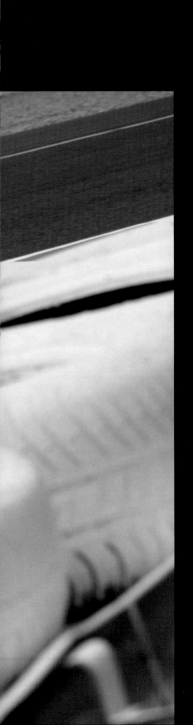

Grand Prix of France

**23 May
Le Mans | France**

▲ We stayed at Jerez for a test and worked a lot on my starts. It paid off at Le Mans and we got away well, maintaining a good rhythm to pass and escape from Pedrosa and Rossi. My first ever back-to-back wins in MotoGP made me the first Spanish rider to do so since Sete Gibernau in 2004 and extended my early advantage at the top of the championship.

Grand Prix of Great Britain
20 June
Silverstone | Great Britain

▲ It may not have been much fun for the fans but Silverstone was without doubt my best performance of the season. In the same way Pedrosa was untouchable at Mugello, this time it was my turn. I was on the limit from the start line to the flag and I don't think I made a single mistake.

Grand Prix of Italy
6 June
Mugello | Italy

◀ You never want to see a rival get hurt and I was sick for Valentino when I saw his crash. Everybody said the championship would be easier because of his injury but Pedrosa's impeccable victory in this race proved that the title would be just as difficult to win with or without the World Champion on track.

Dutch TT
26 June
Assen | Netherlands

▼ In Holland I made it back-to-back wins for the second time that season. I got my Lorenzo's Land flag back out for the celebration just because I hadn't done it for a while and Assen is such a special circuit to me. I planted the flag as if I was a robot because that is what I was trying to be on the bike, not allowing myself negative thoughts that could lead to mistakes.

Grand Prix of Catalunya
4 July
Circuit de Catalunya | Catalunya

▲ At Montmeló I won from pole for the third straight race, becoming the first Yamaha rider to do so since Eddie Lawson in 1986. It was also my seventh podium from the first seven races, putting me into an elite group with seven other '7/7ers': John Surtees, Mike Hailwood, Giacomo Agostini, Wayne Rainey, Mick Doohan, Kevin Schwantz and Valentino Rossi. Not bad company...

18 July
Sachsenring | Germany

I have never had much luck at Sachsenring and this year started out true to form: in practice my engine broke and the resultant oil slick caused Ben Spies and Randy de Puniet to crash. However, things turned around with pole position on Saturday and second place on Sunday despite us not having any dry track practice time and the race being red-flagged and restarted. My crew chief Ramón Forcada and the guys did a great job and as you can see I was delighted with the 20 points.

Grand Prix of United States

25 July
Mazda Raceway | United States

▲ Things got even better at Laguna Seca. It is a circuit I love and for the first time I was able to savour it fully without injuries. Pedrosa, Stoner and I made a break but the pace was so hot that the other two made a couple of mistakes and I was able to escape. It was a bit of a shame because I think we could have seen a nice battle between the three of us but I didn't care – I was going on holiday with a 72-point lead. Even the fact they mistakenly played the Italian anthem on the podium couldn't spoil my mood!

Grand Prix of Czech Republic
 15 August
Automotodrom Brno | Czech Republic

◄ With Valentino having just announced that he would be signing for Ducati the post-race test at Brno was my first as Yamaha's 'lead' rider, as we began work on the 2011 YZR-M1.

▼ Another win I owed to the work of Ramón and the guys, who found an ideal dry set-up for the race even though practice was hit by rain. It allowed me to lead from the front after a couple of early passes on Spies and Pedrosa.

Grand Prix of Indianapolis

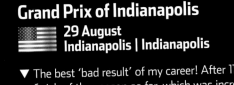

29 August
Indianapolis | Indianapolis

▼ The best 'bad result' of my career! After 11 races third place at Indy was my worst finish of the season so far, which was incredible. It was a tough race because the temperature was more than 35 degrees and the track wasn't in great shape – it was covered in cracks and bumps. I was disappointed because I felt I could have done even better but as the hours passed I took stock and was happy to have scored some very valuable points.

Grand Prix of San Marino

**5 September
Misano | San Marino**

▲ At this point of the season I was starting to get a little anxious because the Yamaha
was beginning to show signs of weakness compared to the Honda and the Ducati:
power, acceleration out of the corners and top speed. At Misano we were clocking
10kph less than the Honda and Pedrosa took his second straight win, a feat he had not
managed since making his MotoGP debut back in 2006. However, the abiding memory
for me, and anyone who was in the paddock that day, is the death of Shoya Tomizawa
in the Moto2 race. Shoya was a great person, a born fighter and a rider with huge
potential. When something like that happens nothing else matters.

Grand Prix of Aragón

19 September
Motorland Aragón | Spain

▼ I trained for two weeks before Aragón like I hadn't trained for a while. I wanted to show that after two races I could be back competing at the front again, in front of my fans at a new and spectacular circuit and, in particular, to dedicate a win to Shoya's family. Unfortunately our bike just wasn't up to the task, especially on the long back straight, and when Nicky beat me to the final podium position on the last lap I screamed with anger.

"For all the statistics and records in 2010 the most important number of all would be on the front of my bike in 2011. The countdown from 99 to 1 was now complete."

Grand Prix of Malaysia

10 October
Sepang Circuit | Malaysia

▲ We were unable to wrap up the title at the first attempt in Japan but in Malaysia our dream finally came true. I had imagined the moment so many times but it was a strange sensation – I didn't really feel anything at the time. The realisation and euphoria would sink in later that evening.

▶ It was the result of a lifetime's work for me, the hard work of the whole team, and just reward for the faith Lin Jarvis (pictured right) had shown in me since first making contact back in 2006.

Grand Prix of Australia

 17 October
Phillip Island | Australia

▼ Racing for the first time as MotoGP World Champion, I felt I could ride more freely and enjoy myself without thinking about the risk of crashing, even though obviously I didn't want to! I finished second but with Casey around that is the best result you can hope for at Phillip Island.

Grand Prix of Valencia

 7 November
Comunitat Valenciana | Valencia

▲ I had almost forgotten what it was like to win but we managed to do it in the final two races at Estoril and Valencia. The points record was a nice bonus but for all the statistics and records in 2010 the most important number of all would be on the front of my bike in 2011. The countdown from 99 to 1 was now complete.

04

Let's celebrate!

Celebrate good times!

I like to have fun with my racing and I like the people at home to have fun too. Some people think I am copying Valentino, the originator of post-race victory celebrations, others feel that I take things too far. Personally I just hope they're accepted for what they are: harmless, innocent fun but always with a

moral to the 'story'. Usually on a Thursday we go for a lap on a couple of scooters – Héctor, Wilco, Carlos and I – and we have a look at what kind of celebration we might be able to do. If we don't get inspiration from the circuit we'll revert to something we might have thought of previously and

do that. I just try to think of celebrations that surprise people, that I have fun with and that the fans enjoy. If I don't manage those three things there is no point. It's weird because whenever we find a place I picture how the celebration could be and usually it is exactly how I imagine it.

▲ It is fantastic to have such a growing legion of fans around the world. My Fan Club dress up as Spartans (above), which is something that really inspires me, and then there is always some crazy fan (below) like this guy in Japan with an idea of his own!

▶ I am a huge FC Barcelona fan so after their victory in the 2009 Champions League Cup Final over Manchester United, which I went to see in Rome, I planted the club flag in the gravel at Montmeló and then proudly wore my shirt at Mugello.

▲ This is my favourite celebration ever, although it almost went badly wrong. My plan was to jump in near the steps but with all the excitement I forgot and must have jumped in 10 or 15 metres away from them. The leathers got heavy as they soaked up the water and I felt I could have drowned...

▶ Probably my second favourite: The Beatles play Silverstone! When we arrived in London we went into a fancy dress shop for a laugh and when I saw the Sergeant Pepper outfits I knew they'd be perfect. It was the most expensive celebration of the season but still cheap compared to the original 'Gladiator' outfit I rented in 2007!

"I just try to think of celebrations that surprise people, that I have fun with and that the fans enjoy."

▼ There were more of my Fan Club at Montmeló than ever before in 2010, all gathered in the G stand, so I promised them I would do my celebration there if I won. I couldn't think of anything new so I drove in the Lorenzo's Land flag in slow motion and they all copied me – it was wonderful!

▼ At Brno I took my seventh win of the season to lead the championship by 77 points. There is a golf course right next to the circuit so sinking a putt on the seventh hole seemed perfect. Except I missed...

▲ The USGP in 2010 was around the same time as the 40th anniversary of the first moon landing, so I thought it would be fun to get the astronaut suit out. I got off the bike in the Corkscrew and ran into an ambulance to change – I was dying laughing! Once I got my helmet back on I pulled the visor down, grabbed the flag and ... stepped out onto the moon.

05

Helmets

More than just a 'skid lid'

A bit like my celebrations, I like to come up with new and funny ideas for my helmets. I think it's something the fans enjoy and I also get a lot of entertainment out of it too – it has become another way of expressing myself. I get inspiration from all kinds of places. The one on the previous page, for instance, came from an episode of 'The Simpsons', where Homer evolves from a monkey to a Neanderthal who spends his life sprawled on the sofa with a beer in his hand. The message is that we can't afford to get too comfortable and we have to constantly work hard to stay in shape. If I think a helmet is lucky sometimes I use it again, like the astronaut helmet from my wins at Estoril. Other times the helmet can be an opportunity to promote a sponsor or a charity. The most important thing, of course, is that it protects your head!

▲ The Spartans logo for my official fan club. I added this design to the back of my standard black helmet at the start of the 2010 season.

◄ (Clockwise from top left) Chupa Chups were an important sponsor in my early career; 'Halo 3: ODST' – one of my favourite games on the X-Box; part of my tribute to FC Barcelona in 2009; the Captain America helmet from Indianapolis – Americans love a superhero!

▲ My long-term association with Chupa Chups ended when I split with my manager at the end of 2008. I had a lot of ideas for a new helmet design, although the 'X-Fuera' logo I designed a few years earlier was the obvious choice!

▶ I wanted Shoya's family to see his helmet on the podium having fought for victory on the track. I wanted him to see his childhood dream come true, the same dream I had: to be one day in MotoGP. Our helmet manufacturers made it possible but unfortunately we weren't able to do it in the race at Aragon.

▲ I wanted to do another special design at Indy after the success of Captain America in 2009. They love their comics and superheroes in the States and these special designs are really popular. I went to an autograph signing session for X-Lite that weekend and the best sellers were Captain America and the astronaut.

I chose the number 99 for the 2009 season partly because it offered a lot of interesting design possibilities, like the 'angel and devil' on my helmet. It reflects both sides of my character. Garmin were a new personal sponsor for 2010.

▲ I 'pimped' my usual helmet for the final round of 2010 at Valenca, having it dipped in gold and encrusted, by hand, with 18,000 Swarovski crystals in the shape of the 'X-Fuera' logo. It took 96 hours to complete and replicas went on sale for €12,000!

◄ (From left) A special design for Japan based on a painting, which also featured kanjis, a dragon and a geisha; showing support for a campaign for blood donors in Barcelona; the top of my special FC Barcelona helmet from 2009.

06

Away from the paddock

Spanish man in New York

▼ After the race at Indianapolis I took the opportunity to visit New York, a city everybody talks about and the setting of countless movies. As a big fan of the movies it was a place I really wanted to see for myself.

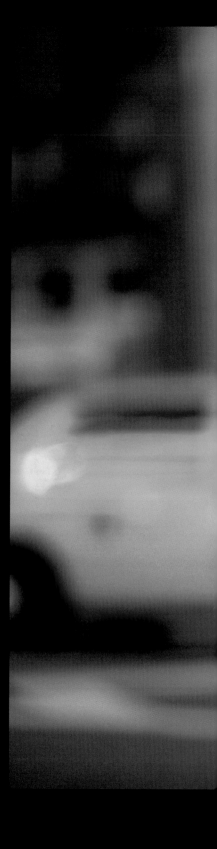

▲ They say New Yorkers are unsociable and it is true, but they are good people. It was nice to walk around and not be recognised. I must admit I like being famous: it's cool to see myself on the covers of magazines and things like that – above all because it means we are doing our job right – but there is another side to it. I can't even go out to a nightclub any more or go for a meal in public without being stopped every five minutes for my picture to be taken. Maybe that's a good thing, it keeps me in check! The good thing is the money and it's easier to pull women!

"It was nice to
walk through New
York without being
recognised"

▲ Even when I'm taking a break I can't put down my mobile phone. I don't remember this photo being taken but there is a good chance I was updating my followers on Twitter about what a great place New York is.

▶ Along with Times Square, Central Park was the place that impressed me most about New York. It is amazing to find such an oasis of calm in the middle of such a chaotic and busy city: a fitting metaphor for the holiday in the midst of a hectic part of the season.

▼ Having dinner at the famous Hard Rock New York. I loved seeing all the memorabilia on the walls and thinking how many movie and rock stars had eaten there in the past.

▲ We spent two nights in a hotel in Times Square and I was really impressed by the whole area. We also went to see the John Lennon tribute in Central Park, which was fantastic.

Amsterdam

▼ Despite my love affair with Assen over the years I had never had the chance to visit Amsterdam, so we finally took the opportunity in 2010 during the week before the Grand Prix. I spent Monday and Tuesday as a tourist, resting in the hotel of an evening but walking the streets of the city during the day.

▲ I think I saw everything there is to see in Amsterdam (by day at least!) and I caught up on plenty of sleep at night. It is important to enjoy life a little away from racing and the trip was a good way to disconnect between back-to-back races at Silverstone and Assen.

▲ With the TVE team (from left, Marc Martin, Alex Crivillé, Izaskun Ruiz, Angel Nieto and Ernest Riveras) at the premiere of 'Jorge', a documentary about my life, in Madrid in December 2010. I was shaking with nerves and excitement all the way through but it was one of the happiest days of my life and I am really satisfied with how the documentary turned out.

Madrid

▼ The screening took place at the Capitol Cinema on Gran Via, Madrid's version of New York's Broadway or London's Leicester Square, and there was a wonderful turnout of fans on the red carpet.

"I was shaking
with nerves and
excitement all the
way through but
it was one of the
happiest days in
my life."

The Sant Josep de la Muntanya orphanage

▲ It was a huge honour this year for me to open a toy library in my name at the Sant Josep de la Muntanya orphanage in Barcelona, which is home to around 70 children between the ages of two and 16. The toy library has table tennis and Scalextric ... all kinds of things that most of us take for granted.

▲It was amazing to see all the kids dressed in my 'X-Fuera' t-shirts and Yamaha caps. I had such great fun with them and the opportunity to spend time with children like this is really priceless. It makes you realise how lucky you are and I promised I'd be back soon – this time for dinner!

Jay Leno's garage

▲ Before going to Indianapolis Yamaha USA took us to Jay Leno's house to see his garage, which is full of classic cars and bikes. His collection is very impressive and as a person he is nice enough, although I remember he didn't look at me much when we spoke. He's a bit of a diva.

Buenafuente

▼The Spanish equivalent of Jay Leno is a guy called Andreu Buenafuente. When I
appeared on his show earlier in 2010 I promised him that I would do something for him
in one of my celebrations. So after the win at Estoril I swapped my usual Lorenzo's Land
flag for one that said 'Buenafuente's Land', with a picture of him in the middle!

'Águila Roja' (TVE)

◄ In 2009 I made a cameo appearance on the Spanish television drama 'Águila Roja'. I played a famous donkey racer and raced against one of the main characters, who had to beat me in order to get money for his poor family. It was good fun but harder than I expected.

► As a child and also early in my racing career I always wanted to become an actor, but not anymore. It's really difficult and I get very nervous. I am not very natural and I would have to spend a lot of time working on my skills. I don't have time, at least not now.

lenge with Rafa Muñoz

celebration at Jerez, TVE set up a fun challenge with the swimmer Rafa
e had a swimming race but with him wearing a set of leathers, helmet, gloves
I was only wearing trunks so I won but he didn't finish that far behind me.
as unbelievable strength – his back is three times as big as mine!

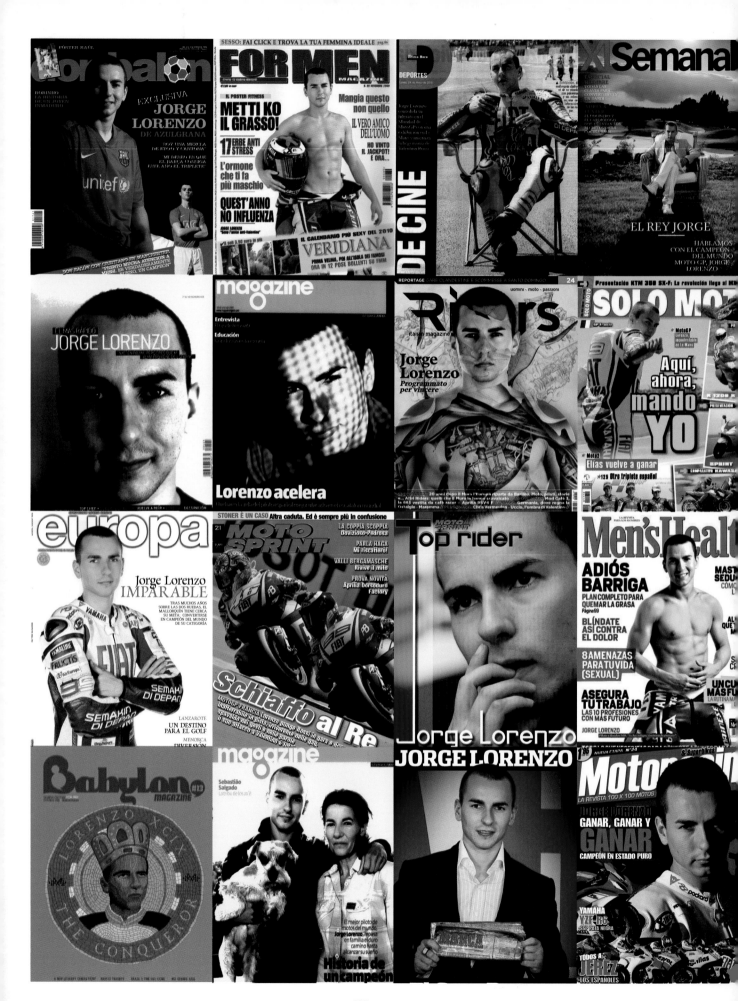

"I must admit I like being famous: it's cool to see myself on the covers of magazines and things like that."

Charity work

I am proud of the charity work that I am able to carry out during each year. Of course, I would always like to do more, but over the course of the season I like to think I add my 'grain of sand' to the cause. As professional sports people I feel we have a responsibility to use our profile in a positive way, to help those less fortunate than ourselves. It also serves as a constant reminder of how lucky we are and keeps our 'problems' in perspective.

Talita 2010

At the end of the 2009 season I took part in a photo shoot for the Talita Foundation's solidarity calendar, an initiative created with the purpose of helping children and young people with Down's Syndrome. Here I am posing with an incredible young girl called Anna Marlasca.

The 'Red Card to abuse' campaign, launched by the Ministry of Equality in Spain

▲ This is a cause I felt strongly about taking part in. I wanted to show the red card to all those who use their physical strength to abuse others, but specifically in this case women. I will always endeavour to eradicate violence in our society.

A tear for Africa

▲ This photo was part of an exhibition called 'Una lágrima por África' by a photojournalist called Joan Valls, and footballers Lionel Messi, Carles Puyol, Raul Tamudo and Carlos Kameni were also featured. The originals were sold off to raise money for relief projects that Kameni works with in his home country of Cameroon.

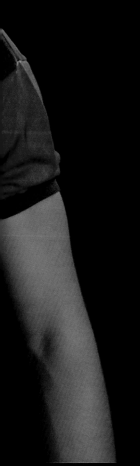

Give blood

▼ I added an extra sticker to my helmet for the Catalunya GP in 2010 as part of a campaign to promote giving blood in Barcelona. As it is an important global message I made the sticker in English, with the blue cross – the new international symbol of blood donation.

▼ This didn't go down well. I just did it as a simple gesture of support to an injured colleague and team-mate but he saw it as me poking fun at him or trying to win over his fans. I was disappointed but at least I know not to do it again. I would for any other rider – like I did for de Puniet at Laguna Seca. But for Valentino? Never again.

▲ Helping out my friend Xavi Vallejo, who runs a riding school. They teach people how to ride on the road, although perhaps this photo isn't the best example! I guess I was showing them what NOT to do...

◄ I did quite a bit of work on road safety campaigns in 2010, including patrolling the roads around Montmeló with Catalunya traffic police and handing out leaflets during the F1 Grand Prix. It was a great experience. I am getting very sensible in my old age.

The Sant Josep de la Muntanya children's home

◀ It was great to be able to welcome the kids from the Sant Josep de la Muntanya children's home into my garage at Montmeló. They are normal children who want to have fun, and these moments when they see their idols are exciting for them.

Yago

▼ Yago was a very special visitor to my garage at Valencia in 2010. He had a serious illness that needed constant attention but he was able to come down from his home in Galicia, which is also where my father is from, with his sister and parents. Seeing his strength of character gave me extra motivation for the race.

Back to my roots

◀ My relationship with my father is back on track now after our well documented problems and I get back to Mallorca whenever I can to help him out with his riding school.

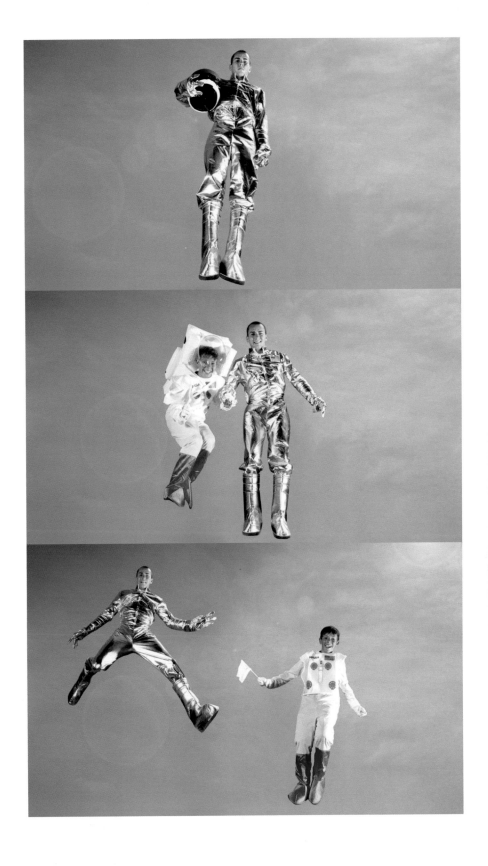

ANIMA Foundation Calendar 2011

▲ Posing for a photo with Pol from the children's home for the Ànima Foundation 2011 calendar. The idea here is simple: if you can dream it, it is possible. My becoming MotoGP World Champion proves it, and it is an important message to these kids. I also took part in the 2009 calendar.

◀ This was the exact same suit that I took to Laguna Seca for my post-race celebration!

"The idea here
is simple: if you
can dream it,
it is possible."

07

My friends

(From top) With Marcos Hirsch – my personal trainer, manager and soul mate; Ricky Cardús – my best friend, training partner and one of the few people who understands me; Valerio Fumagalli and Carlos Gil – a.k.a. Luigi and Mario!

▲ Never far from my side is Héctor Martín, who is officially my press officer but also helps deal with my day-to-day affairs. We met back in 2004 when he interviewed me for *Diario de Mallorca* and we have been close friends ever since. I have lots of nicknames for him including 'El Caniche' (The Poodle), Gremlin and Mike (because he looks like di Meglio)!

The circle of trust

I am lucky that I get to meet a lot of people through my work but in my position it is difficult to know who you can trust. Experience has taught me this much. Thankfully I have built a small circle of friends who I know are always by my side. They look after my professional and personal interests and always seek to put me first. Thanks to them, I am able to do my job properly in the knowledge that I always have somebody close by to turn to during the difficult times.

"I have built a small circle of friends who I know are always by my side."

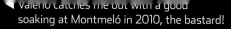

▲ Long-haul races are boring because we don't have our motorhome so we spend a lot of time on the internet. Here I am with Marcos in Australia – it must be after the race because you can see my bottle of cava for finishing second is on the table!

08

My fans

▲ I get asked to sign some strange things but a policeman's helmet during our World Champion's reception in Palma de Mallorca was one of the most unusual! We were followed on a parade through the city by 3,000 bikers – it was an unforgettable day.

Giving something back

I have worked hard over the years on how my image is portrayed because in the past I have come across as arrogant or distant from the fans. More and more I feel I am being appreciated and I like to give

them something back whenever I can, whether it is an invitation to my Fan Club dinner or a short message on Twitter. The public give me so much and it is nice to be able to return the favour, albeit in a small way.

▼ I am always amazed how enthusiastic and polite the fans are in America. It is one of my favourite countries to go to and I have no problem spending time signing autographs at Laguna Seca or Indianapolis – two of my favourite circuits on the calendar.

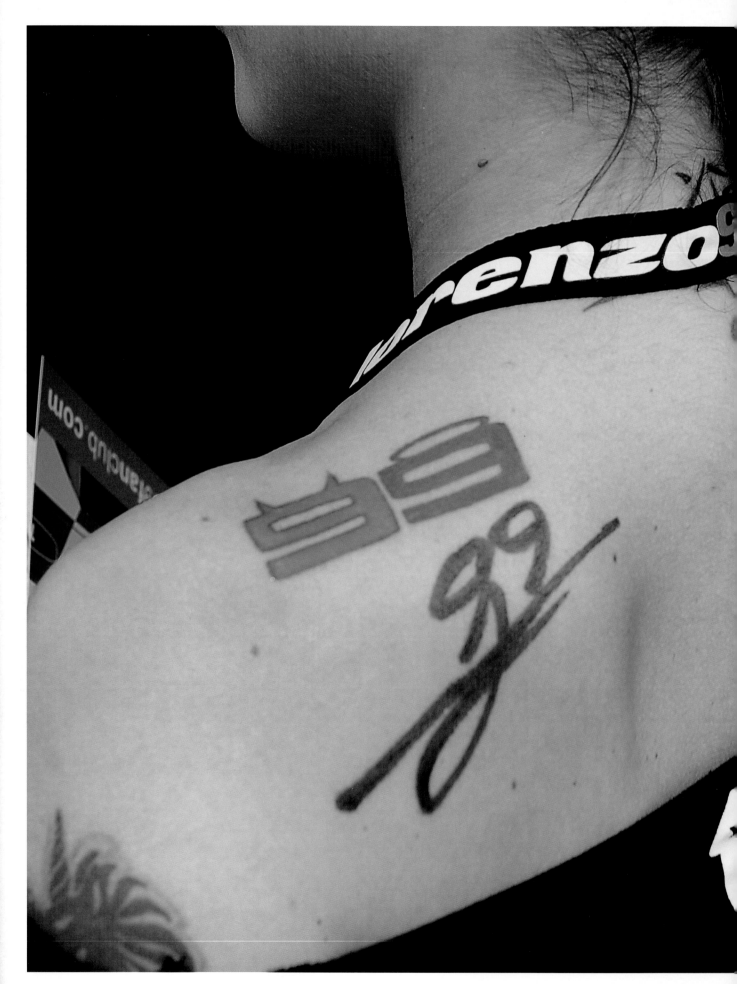

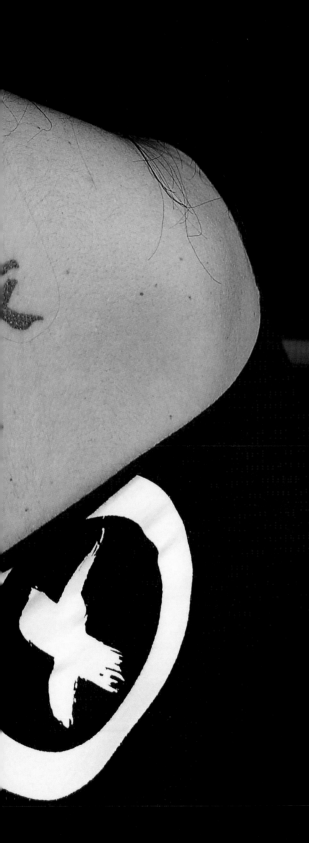

"I found it quite weird that she had the tattoo – especially since I don't even have one myself."

◀ It is nice to be wanted by the public. I think their perception of me has changed over the years and I am pleased because I want to be remembered not only as a successful rider but one who was well liked by the fans.

▼ One of the my strongest followings is building in the UK, where I have a special relationship with the fans – I think partly because I lived there for a while. Day of Champions is one of my favourite events of the year. Indonesia is another country with a lot of fans.

◀ I had a dinner for 200 members of my Fan Club on my return to Barcelona after winning the title. On the far left I am signing the shoulder of a girl with the 99 tattoo on her back. I found it quite weird that she had the tattoo – especially since I don't even have one myself.

09

Life through a lens

I don't usually make this much noise in hotel rooms, I promise! The people in the room below must have wondered what was going on! The suit was ruined but at least it wasn't mine.

Taking instructions is not something I am used to but posing for photos like this is harder than it looks. I have to admit, though, I don't mind posing so it wasn't too much of a chore.

FHM magazine

Three photographers (Mirco Lazzari, Max and Douglas) and their assistant, two of the bosses from Getty Images, a stylist, a make-up artist, a press officer, a director from *FHM*, a graphics editor from *FHM*, a video cameraman, PR representatives from Moët et Chandon and Xbox, a maintenance guy to adjust the air conditioning and a waitress from room service... all packed into a suite at the Juan Carlos I Hotel in Barcelona! And in the middle of all that I am jumping around in an expensive suit! I guess it is nice to have the opportunity to do something different...

"The suit was
ruined but at least
it wasn't mine."

▲ I don't envy full-time models. The days are long and I can imagine it is hard to continually try to look your best when you are feeling tired or unhappy.

▶ This is a familiar scene for me – reading magazines and watching television in a hotel room. But I don't usually look so smart.

▼ Each shot captures only a moment in time but they don't reflect the hours of preparation and hanging around that go into it.

▲ I'm definitely more comfortable in a leather jacket, jeans and sunglasses than I am in a full dinner suit and black tie.

◄ The late summer sun at Misano created a dramatic light for these shots, which were taken on the Wednesday ahead of the race, before the crates were unpacked following their delivery from Indianapolis.

Riders magazine

Riders is a high-class Italian publication. They always try to do things a little differently and it's always a pleasure to speak with them and do some photos. They came to Misano in 2010 to take some shots and do an interview – I actually appeared on the front cover of this issue, as you can see back on page 182 of this book. You will see what I mean about them doing things differently.

"I don't envy
full-time models.
The days are
long and I can
imagine it is hard
to continually try
to look your best
when you are
feeling tired
or unhappy."

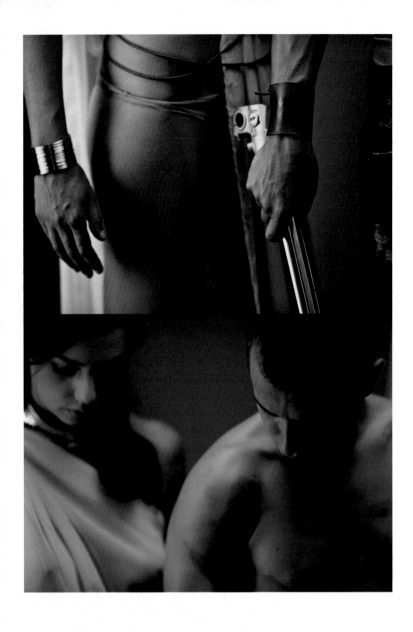

▲ Taking some time out between shots and between clothing rails to send a quick text message.

◀ I like to think I am a good professional but I must admit it is difficult to concentrate on anything when you have a semi-naked woman standing right behind you!

Barracuda calendar

For the last couple of years I have been featured in the annual calendar of Barracuda, who sell motorcycling accessories. They always seem to have me taking my clothes off next to a very hot female model. Never mind the last few laps of a race – it is times like this when the hard work Marcos and I put in at the gym really counts!

"Never mind the last few laps of a race – it is times like this when the hard work Marcos and I put in in the gym really counts!"

▲ Even though I am no expert in photography I like to get involved in every stage of the process of any project I am involved in and make sure I am happy with the outcome before it is published.

▲ Time for a quick break in between shoots. There's nothing like a traditional Spanish 'bikini' – a toasted ham and cheese sandwich. I don't get to eat many of these during the season.

▶ With the shoot completed I finally get to put on my own jacket and head home. It has been good fun and a nice change, but I would rather spend my day working out at the gym or on a bike, that's for sure.

▼ Alpinestars have been winning titles for a long time, with some of my heroes like Kenny Roberts Sr from back in his days racing dirt-track in the USA.

Alpinestars

After several years with Dainese I signed up with Alpinestars for 2011. They will provide my leathers, boots and gloves for the new season and I am really pleased. They make great equipment, they're a really cool company and their slogan sums up my approach to racing: one goal, one vision.

▲ One of the first things I did for Alpinestars was a video interview for their website with former 250cc Grand Prix rider Jamie Robinson, who now works as a journalist.

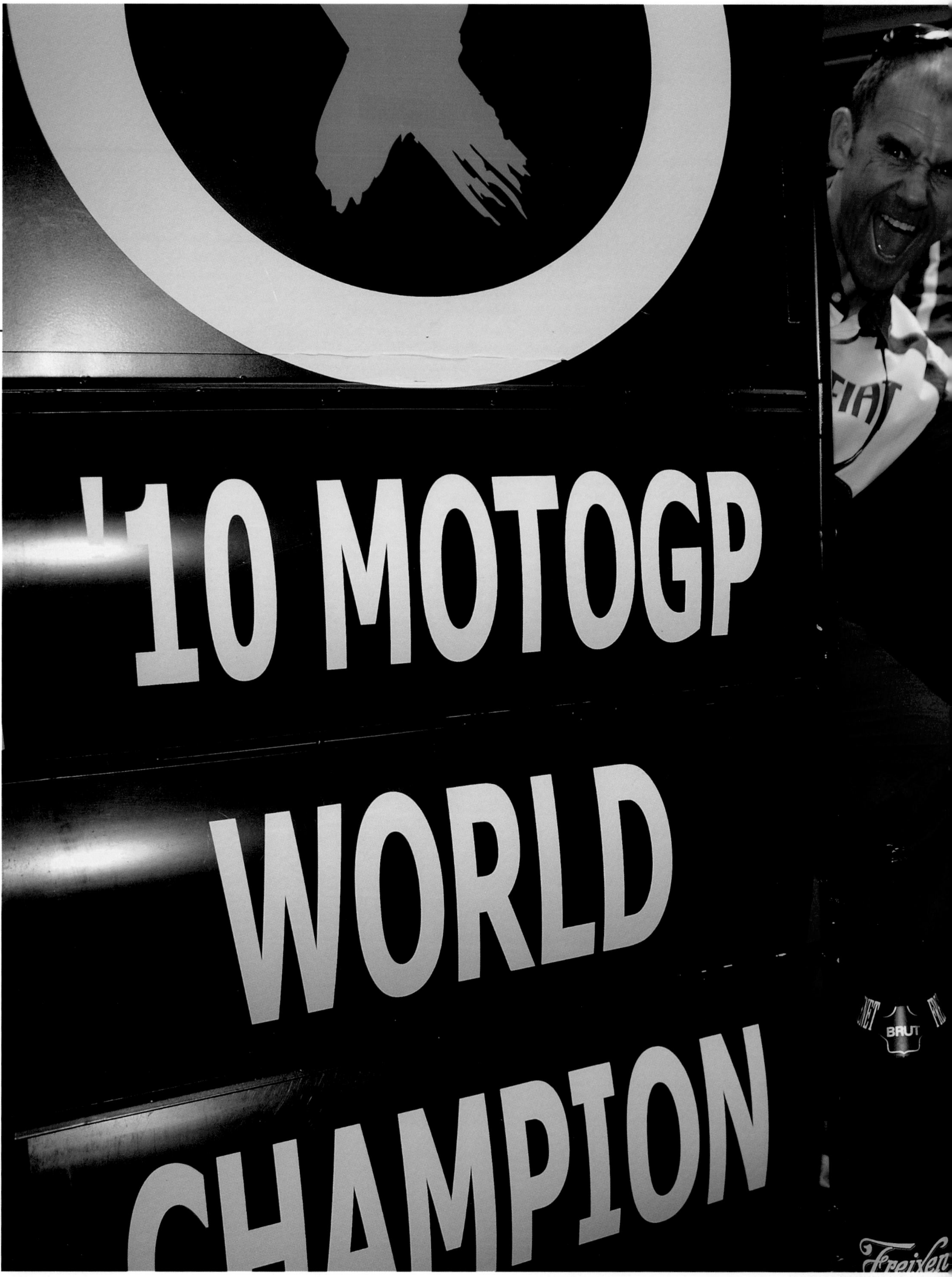
'10 MOTOGP
WORLD
CHAMPION
FIAT
BRUT

MotoGP World Champion

Finally time to take it easy

Once my professional commitments were out of the way for 2010 I was finally able to soak up the feeling of being 2010 MotoGP World Champion and enjoy myself for a little while. I spent time with my family in Mallorca and at home in Barcelona, where I was able to share my success with all the people who had supported me throughout the year and my career in general.

It was a great honour to be given an award by the Spanish sports newspaper *AS*, especially in such a great year for sport in our country – in particular the national football team winning the World Cup. It was also a great year for my fellow Mallorcan Rafa Nadal, who won three slams and regained the world number one spot in tennis.

▲ At the end of November I was invited onto the pitch at the famous Nou Camp stadium ahead of Barcelona's 'El Clasico' derby match against Real Madrid. It was a huge honour for me and I got a great ovation from the fans. Also Barcelona won 5–0 so it couldn't have been better!

◄ This was during a live recording of a concert by the Spanish band 'El Canto del Loco' on the radio station Cadena Ser. I joined in with the lead singer Dani Martín but I don't think they'll be asking me to join the band.

Govern
de les Illes Balea

"It was also a great year for my fellow Mallorcan Rafa Nadal, who won three slams and regained the world number one spot in tennis."

▼ In December I was invited on a popular Spanish television show called 'El Hormiguero', which literally means 'The Anthill'. It is a bit wacky and I had fun. From the top: giving Pablo Motos (host of the programme) a surprise when he saw me appearing with a wig; chatting with the crazy puppets Barrancas and Trancas; making chocolate brownies in a time challenge!

▲ Traditionally the Barcelona Aquarium ask a sports star to celebrate Christmas and the New Year by scuba diving in their tanks and at the end of 2010 they asked me! I swam with 80 different species of fish and with sharks measuring over three metres in length. As you can see I planted a flag at the bottom of the tank that read 'Lorenzo's Sea' as opposed to my usual 'Lorenzo's Land'. I felt pretty comfortable in there because on the track I am used to swimming with sharks – in fact ever since I arrived in MotoGP there has been a great white in my tank! It was an unforgettable way to finish an unforgettable year.